Pebble®

GREAT HISPANIC AND LATINO AMERICANS

Sonia Sotomayor

by Erika L. Shores

CAPSTONE PRESS
a capstone imprint

D0101486

Pebble Books are published by Capstone Press,
1710 Roe Crest Drive, North Mankato, Minnesota 56003
www.mycapstone.com

Library of Congress Cataloging-in-Publication Data
Names: Shores, Erika L., 1976– author.
Title: Sonia Sotomayor / By Erika L. Shores.
Description: North Mankato, Minnesota : Capstone Press, 2017. | Series: Pebble
books. Great Hispanic and Latino Americans. | Includes bibliographical references
and index. Identifiers: LCCN 2016005745| ISBN 9781515732594 (library binding) |
ISBN 9781515732600 (pbk.) | ISBN 9781515732617 (eBook pdf)
Subjects: LCSH: Sotomayor, Sonia, 1954– | Hispanic American judges—Biography. |
Judges—United States—Biography.
Classification: LCC KF8745.S67 .S56 2017 | DDC 347.73/2634—dc23
LC record available at http://lccn.loc.gov/2016005745

Note to Parents and Teachers

The Great Hispanic and Latino Americans series supports national
curriculum standards for social studies related to people, places,
and culture. This book describes and illustrates Sonia Sotomayor.
The images support early readers in understanding the text. The
repetition of words and phrases helps early readers learn new
words. This book also introduces early readers to subject-specific
vocabulary words, which are defined in the Glossary section. Early
readers may need assistance to read some words and to use the
Table of Contents, Glossary, Read More, Internet Sites, and Index
sections of the book.

Printed in the United States of America in North Mankato, Minnesota.
009663F16

Table of Contents

1954
born

About Sonia

Sonia Sotomayor is a
U.S. Supreme Court justice.
She is the first Hispanic
to hold this important job.
She was born June 25, 1954,
in the Bronx, New York.

The U.S. Supreme Court is the most
powerful court in the United States.
Nine justices make up this court.

Young Sonia
with her parents

1954
born

Sonia's parents, Celina and Juan, grew up in Puerto Rico. They met after moving to New York City. Many of their family members moved to New York too.

Sonia was close to her grandmother, cousins, aunts, and uncles.

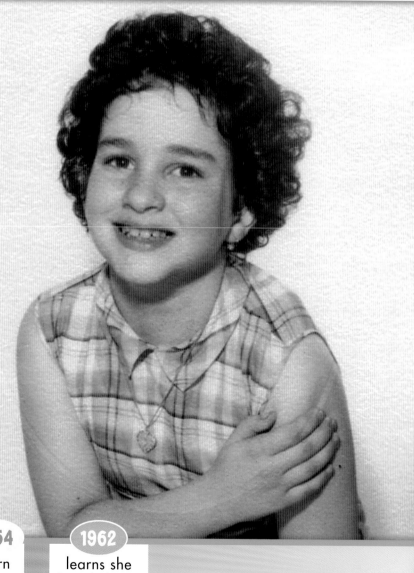

1954
born

1962
learns she
has diabetes

At age 7, Sonia found out she had type 1 diabetes. Her blood had too much sugar in it. She had to take medicine to control it. Sonia learned how to give herself the shots.

Sonia with her mother in 2009

1954	1962	1963
born	learns she has diabetes	her father dies

Sonia's life changed again
when her father died in 1963.
Celina had to work hard.
She paid for private school for
Sonia and Sonia's brother,
Juan Junior. Celina wanted her
children to have a good education.

Sonia at her eighth
grade graduation

1954
born

1962
learns she
has diabetes

1963
her father
dies

Sonia was smart. She loved reading and math. She read *Nancy Drew* mysteries. Sonia also watched TV shows about lawyers. She set a goal to become a lawyer or a judge someday.

1954	1962	1963	1976
born	learns she has diabetes	her father dies	graduates from Princeton

14

Lawyer and Judge

After high school, Sonia went to Princeton University. It was a big step. Sonia was the first in her family to go to such a highly respected school. Sonia was a top student at Princeton.

Sonia by her office window
in New York in 1998

| **1954** | **1962** | **1963** | **1976** |
| born | learns she has diabetes | her father dies | graduates from Princeton |

Sonia went to Yale Law School.

In 1979 Sonia became a lawyer

for the state of New York.

She worked very hard.

Many people respected her.

In 1992 she was chosen

to be a judge.

1979
becomes
a lawyer

1992
selected
to be a
judge

Sonia with President Obama

1954	**1962**	**1963**	**1976**
born	learns she has diabetes	her father dies	graduates from Princeton

Sonia's Life Today

As a judge, Sonia was tough but fair. She earned even greater respect. In 2009 President Barack Obama named Sonia to the Supreme Court. She became only the third woman to serve on the court.

1979	1992	2009
becomes a lawyer	selected to be a judge	named to the U.S. Supreme Court

1954
born

1962
learns she
has diabetes

1963
her father
dies

1976
graduates
from
Princeton

Sonia wrote *My Beloved World* in 2013. She tells of her life and the challenges she's faced. Sonia believes that hard work and courage can make dreams come true.

1979	1992	2009	2013
becomes a lawyer	selected to be a judge	named to the U.S. Supreme Court	writes a book about her life

Glossary

challenge—something that is hard to do

courage—to show bravery

court—a place where laws are carried out; also, a gathering headed by a judge or judges

diabetes—a disease in which there is too much sugar in the blood

goal—something that you aim for or work toward

Hispanic—a person of Mexican, South American, or other Spanish-speaking background

judge—a person appointed to decide cases in a court of law

lawyer—a person who is trained to advise people about the law and who acts and speaks for them in court

respect—to believe in the quality and worth of someone or something

Read More

Kramer, Barbara. *National Geographic Kids Readers: Sonia Sotomayor*. Washington, D.C.: National Geographic, 2016.

McPherson, Stephanie Sammartino. *Sonia Sotomayor: Supreme Court Justice*. Exceptional Latinos. New York: Enslow Publishers, 2016.

Williams, Zella. *Sonia Sotomayor: Supreme Court Justice*. Hispanic Headliners. New York: PowerKids Press, 2011.

Internet Sites

FactHound offers a safe, fun way to find Internet sites related to this book. All of the sites on FactHound have been researched by our staff.

Here's all you do:

Visit *www.facthound.com*

Type in this code: 9781515732594

Check out projects, games and lots more at
www.capstonekids.com

Index

Editorial Credits

Charmaine Whitman, designer; Kelly Garvin, media researcher;
Tori Abraham, production specialist

Photo Credits

AP Images/Mark Lennihan, 16; Corbis/Ron Sachs/CNP, 4; Newscom: Dennis Brack,
18, Handout/MCT, cover, 1, 20, POOL/Rueters, 10, White House/UPI, 6, 8, 12, 14
Artistic Elements: Shutterstock: Eliks, nalinn, tuulijumala